A Daily Prayer Journal

Woman at the Well Ministries

A DAILY PRAYER JOURNAL

ISBN (978-0-9794872-2-4)

Printed in USA by 48HrBooks (www.48HrBooks.com)

WHO YOU ARE

You are a sinner saved by grace, so loved by the Creator that He gave His only Son for you; so loved by the Saviour that He gave His life for you; so important to God that He put Himself into you in the form of the Holy Spirit; so important to the Holy Spirit that He speaks to you; so important to the Kingdom that God has promised to complete the good work He has begun in you; so important to the Trinity that they watch over your every move and make great plans for you.

January 1
Living a Blessed Life

"Blessed are the undefiled in the way, who walk in the law of the Lord."

Psalm 119:1

Prayer Requests:

Answered Prayers:

Thoughts:

January 2
Jesus, My Hiding Place

"Thou art my hiding place and my shield: I hope in thy word."

Psalm 119:114

Prayer Requests:

Answered Prayers:

Thoughts:

January 3
Filled With the Fullness of God

"That He would grant you, according to the riches of His glory, to be strengthened with might by His Spirit in the inner man; That Christ may dwell in your hearts by faith; that ye, being rooted and grounded in love, may be able to comprehend with all saints what is the breadth, and length, and depth, and height; And to know the love of Christ, which passeth knowledge, that ye might be filled with all the fulness of God."

Ephesians 3:16-19

Prayer Requests:

Answered Prayers:

Thoughts:

January 4
Trust in the Lord to Help You

"Ye that fear the Lord, trust in the Lord: He is their help and their shield."

Psalm 115:11

Prayer Requests:

Answered Prayers:

Thoughts:

January 5
Ask, Seek and Knock

"And I say unto you, Ask, and it shall be given you; seek, and ye shall find; knock, and it shall be opened unto you. For every one that asketh receiveth; and he that seeketh findeth; and to him that knocketh it shall be opened."

Luke 11:9-10

Prayer Requests:

Answered Prayers:

Thoughts:

January 6
Why Worry?

"And why take ye thought for raiment? Consider the lilies of the field, how they grow; they toil not, neither do they spin: And yet I say unto you, that even Solomon in all his glory was not arrayed like one of these."

Matthew 6:28-29

Prayer Requests:

Answered Prayers:

Thoughts:

January 7
Time Well Spent

"But without faith it is impossible to please Him: for he that cometh to God must believe that He is, and that He is a rewarder of them that diligently seek Him."

Hebrews 11:6

Prayer Requests:

Answered Prayers:

Thoughts:

January 8
A Time for All Things

"To every thing there is a season, and a time to every purpose under the heaven:"

Ecclesiastes 3:1

Prayer Requests:

Answered Prayers:

Thoughts:

January 9
Each Day Is Important

"So teach us to number our days, that we may apply our hearts unto wisdom."

Psalm 90:12

Prayer Requests:

Answered Prayers:

Thoughts:

January 10
A Time to Witness

"Walk in wisdom toward them that are without, redeeming the time."

Colossians 4:5

Prayer Requests:

Answered Prayers:

Thoughts:

January 11
Love Costs

"My little children, let us not love in word, neither in tongue; but in deed and in truth."

I John 3:18

Prayer Requests:

Answered Prayers:

Thoughts:

January 12
Love Goes the Distance

"We love Him, because He first loved us."

I John 4:19

Prayer Requests:

Answered Prayers:

Thoughts:

January 13
Faith Makes Him Visible

"Now faith is the substance of things hoped for, the evidence of things not seen."

Hebrews 11:1

Prayer Requests:

Answered Prayers:

Thoughts:

January 14
Innocent

"My God hath sent His angel, and hath shut the lions' mouths, that they have not hurt me: forasmuch as before Him innocency was found in me; and also before thee, O king, have I done no hurt."

Daniel 6:22

Prayer Requests:

Answered Prayers:

Thoughts:

January 15
Feathers from Heaven

"He shall cover thee with His feathers, and under His wings shalt thou trust: His truth shall be thy shield and buckler."

Psalm 91:4

Prayer Requests:

Answered Prayers:

Thoughts:

January 16
He Is Able

"If it be so, our God whom we serve is able to deliver us from the burning fiery furnace, and He will deliver us out of thine hand, O king."

Daniel 3:17

Prayer Requests:

Answered Prayers:

Thoughts:

January 17
Promises, Promises, Promises

"And being fully persuaded that, what He had promised, He was able also to perform."

Romans 4:21

Prayer Requests:

Answered Prayers:

Thoughts:

January 18
Separate but Not Apart

"Father, I will that they also, whom Thou hast given me, be with me where I am; that they may behold my glory, which Thou hast given me: for Thou lovedst me before the foundation of the world."

John 17:24

Prayer Requests:

Answered Prayers:

Thoughts:

January 19
He Is Near

"Thou art near, O Lord; and all Thy commandments are truth."

Psalm 119:151

Prayer Requests:

Answered Prayers:

Thoughts:

January 20
Paid In Full

"And walk in love, as Christ also hath loved us, and hath given Himself for us an offering and a sacrifice to God for a sweet smelling savour."

Ephesians 5:2

Prayer Requests:

Answered Prayers:

Thoughts:

January 21
You Are Chosen

"Ye have not chosen Me, but I have chosen you, and ordained you, that ye should go and bring forth fruit, and that your fruit should remain: that whatsoever ye shall ask of the Father in My name, He may give it you."

John 15:16

Prayer Requests:

Answered Prayers:

Thoughts:

January 22
Want to Live Forever

"And this is life eternal, that they might know Thee the only true God, and Jesus Christ, whom Thou hast sent."

John 17:3

Prayer Requests:

Answered Prayers:

Thoughts:

January 23
Why Is There a Bible?

"But these are written, that ye might believe that Jesus is the Christ, the Son of God; and that believing ye might have life through His name."

John 20:31

Prayer Requests:

Answered Prayers:

Thoughts:

January 24
The Value of Faith

"Jesus saith unto him, Thomas, because thou hast seen Me, thou hast believed: blessed are they that have not seen, and yet have believed."

John 20:29

Prayer Requests:

Answered Prayers:

Thoughts:

January 25
Jesus Prays for Us

"I pray for them: I pray not for the world, but for them which Thou hast given me; for they are thine."

John 17:9

Prayer Requests:

Answered Prayers:

Thoughts:

January 26
He Has Sent You

"As thou hast sent me into the world, even so have I also sent them into the world."

John 17:18

Prayer Requests:

Answered Prayers:

Thoughts:

January 27
Christ Is On the Scene

"But He saith unto them, It is I; be not afraid."

John 6:20

Prayer Requests:

Answered Prayers:

Thoughts:

January 28
You Were Made Exactly As He Wanted You

"The Spirit of God hath made me, and the breath of the Almighty hath given me life."

Job 33:4

Prayer Requests:

Answered Prayers:

Thoughts:

January 29
Be Careful What You Speak

"My words shall be of the uprightness of my heart: and my lips shall utter knowledge clearly."

Job 33:3

Prayer Requests:

Answered Prayers:

Thoughts:

January 30
You Belong

"And all that believed were together, and had all things common;"

Acts 2:44

Prayer Requests:

Answered Prayers:

Thoughts:

January 31
Learn While You Are Young

"O God, thou hast taught me from my youth: and hitherto have I declared thy wondrous works."

Psalm 71:17

Prayer Requests:

Answered Prayers:

Thoughts:

February 1
Your Life Is Read By Many

"Then the king commanded, and they brought Daniel, and cast him into the den of lions. Now the king spake and said unto Daniel, Thy God whom thou servest continually, He will deliver thee."

Daniel 6:16

Prayer Requests:

Answered Prayers:

Thoughts:

February 2
Friends Are a Gift from God

"A man that hath friends must shew himself friendly: and there is a friend that sticketh closer than a brother."

Proverbs 18:24

Prayer Requests:

Answered Prayers:

Thoughts:

.

February 3
Hear His Voice

"Hear attentively the noise of His voice, and the sound that goeth out of His mouth."

Job 37:2

Prayer Requests:

Answered Prayers:

Thoughts:

February 4
Knowledge Is A Precious Jewel

"There is gold, and a multitude of rubies: but the lips of knowledge are a precious jewel."

Proverbs 20:15

Prayer Requests:

Answered Prayers:

Thoughts:

February 5
Lead The Way To God

"And this stone, which I have set for a pillar, shall be God's house: and of all that thou shalt give me I will surely give the tenth unto Thee." "Bring ye all the tithes into the storehouse, that there may be meat in mine house, and prove me now herewith, saith the Lord of hosts, if I will not open you the windows of heaven, and pour you out a blessing, that there shall not be room enough to receive it."

Genesis 28:22, Malachi 3:10

Prayer Requests:

Answered Prayers:

Thoughts:

February 6
Going For The Gold

"But He knoweth the way that I take: when He hath tried me, I shall come forth as gold. My foot hath held His steps, His way have I kept, and not declined. Neither have I gone back from the commandment of His lips; I have esteemed the words of His mouth more than my necessary food."

Job 23:10-12

Prayer Requests:

Answered Prayers:

Thoughts:

February 7
Know His Word

"Jesus answered and said unto them, Ye do err, not knowing the scriptures, nor the power of God."

Matthew 22:29

Prayer Requests:

Answered Prayers:

Thoughts:

February 8
Be Thankful

"Giving thanks always for all things unto God and the Father in the name of our Lord Jesus Christ;"

Ephesians 5:20

Prayer Requests:

Answered Prayers:

Thoughts:

February 9
Forgiveness

"Confess your faults one to another, and pray one for another, that ye may be healed. The effectual fervent prayer of a righteous man availeth much."

James 5:16

Prayer Requests:

Answered Prayers:

Thoughts:

February 10
Jesus, Our Friend

"So when they had dined, Jesus saith to Simon Peter, Simon, son of Jonas, lovest thou me more than these? He saith unto Him, Yea, Lord; Thou knowest that I love Thee. He saith unto him, Feed my lambs."

John 21:15

Prayer Requests:

Answered Prayers:

Thoughts:

February 11
God Shines In Your Heart

"For God, who commanded the light to shine out of darkness, hath shined in our hearts, to give the light of the knowledge of the glory of God in the face of Jesus Christ."

II Corinthians 4:6

Prayer Requests:

Answered Prayers:

Thoughts:

February 12
God Is Your Bodyguard

"But the Lord is with me as a mighty terrible one: therefore my persecutors shall stumble, and they shall not prevail: they shall be greatly ashamed; for they shall not prosper: their everlasting confusion shall never be forgotten."

Jeremiah 20:11

Prayer Requests:

Answered Prayers:

Thoughts:

February 13
What a Mighty Warrior You Are

"Ye have not chosen Me, but I have chosen you, and ordained you, that ye should go and bring forth fruit, and that your fruit should remain: that whatsoever ye shall ask of the Father in My name, He may give it you."

John 15:16

Prayer Requests:

Answered Prayers:

Thoughts:

February 14
Heavenly Love

"Greater love hath no man than this, that a man lay down his life for his friends."

John 15:13

Prayer Requests:

Answered Prayers:

Thoughts:

February 15
The Gift of Peace

"Peace I leave with you, My peace I give unto you: not as the world giveth, give I unto you. Let not your heart be troubled, neither let it be afraid."

John 14:27

Prayer Requests:

Answered Prayers:

Thoughts:

February 16
That's Him

"I have heard of Thee by the hearing of the ear: but now mine eye seeth Thee."

Job 42:5

Prayer Requests:

Answered Prayers:

Thoughts:

February 17
Dispatched by God

"Also I heard the voice of the Lord, saying, Whom shall I send, and who will go for us? Then said I, Here am I; send me."

Isaiah 6:8

Prayer Requests:

Answered Prayers:

Thoughts:

February 18
Treasures Unseen

"But lay up for yourselves treasures in heaven, where neither moth nor rust doth corrupt, and where thieves do not break through nor steal:"

Matthew 6:20

Prayer Requests:

Answered Prayers:

Thoughts:

February 19
Acts of Kindness

"But after that the kindness and love of God our Saviour toward man appeared,"

Titus 3:4

Prayer Requests:

Answered Prayers:

Thoughts:

February 20
Just Do It

"Now therefore perform the doing of it; that as there was a readiness to will, so there may be a performance also out of that which ye have."

II Corinthians 8:11

Prayer Requests:

Answered Prayers:

Thoughts:

February 21
He Is Everywhere

"If I ascend up into heaven, Thou art there: if I make my bed in hell, behold, Thou art there. If I take the wings of the morning, and dwell in the uttermost parts of the sea; Even there shall Thy hand lead me, and Thy right hand shall hold me."

Psalm 139:8-10

Prayer Requests:

Answered Prayers:

Thoughts:

February 22
Nothing but Pink Skies for You

"He answered and said unto them, When it is evening, ye say, It will be fair weather: for the sky is red."

Matthew 16:2

Prayer Requests:

Answered Prayers:

Thoughts:

February 23
Knit by the Father's Hands

"That their hearts might be comforted, being knit together in love, and unto all riches of the full assurance of understanding, to the acknowledgement of the mystery of God, and of the Father, and of Christ;"

Colossians 2:2

Prayer Requests:

Answered Prayers:

Thoughts:

February 24
Divided We Fall, United We Stand

"For the Lord God will help me; therefore shall I not be confounded: therefore have I set my face like a flint, and I know that I shall not be ashamed. He is near that justifieth me; who will contend with me? Let us stand together: who is mine adversary? Let him come near to me."

Isaiah 50:7-8

Prayer Requests:

Answered Prayers:

Thoughts:

February 25
Yes, We Should Be Committed Christians

"Commit thy works unto the Lord, and thy thoughts shall be established"

Proverbs 16:3

Prayer Requests:

Answered Prayers:

Thoughts:

February 26

Happy Days

"This is the day which the Lord hath made; we will rejoice and be glad in it."

Psalm 118:24

Prayer Requests:

Answered Prayers:

Thoughts:

February 27
We Are Family

"For whosoever shall do the will of my Father which is in heaven, the same is my brother, and sister, and mother."

Matthew 12:50

Prayer Requests:

Answered Prayers:

Thoughts:

February 28
A Faith that Speaks

"That the communication of thy faith may become effectual by the acknowledging of every good thing which is in you in Christ Jesus."

Philemon 1:6

Prayer Requests:

Answered Prayers:

Thoughts:

March 1
Saved from Sin and Set for Life

"Who gave Himself for us, that He might redeem us from all iniquity, and purify unto Himself a peculiar people, zealous of good works."

Titus 2:14

Prayer Requests:

Answered Prayers:

Thoughts:

March 2
Love Beyond Decree

"Behold, what manner of love the Father hath bestowed upon us, that we should be called the sons of God: therefore the world knoweth us not, because it knew him not."

I John 3:1

Prayer Requests:

Answered Prayers:

Thoughts:

March 3
Refiner's Fire

"Every man's work shall be made manifest: for the day shall declare it, because it shall be revealed by fire; and the fire shall try every man's work of what sort it is."

I Corinthians 3:13

Prayer Requests:

Answered Prayers:

Thoughts:

March 4
Looking for An Adventure

"But as it is written, Eye hath not seen, nor ear heard, neither have entered into the heart of man, the things which God hath prepared for them that love him."

I Corinthians 2:9

Prayer Requests:

Answered Prayers:

Thoughts:

March 5
Sacrificing Self for the Sake of the Brethren

"We then that are strong ought to bear the infirmities of the weak, and not to please ourselves."

Romans 15:1

Prayer Requests:

Answered Prayers:

Thoughts:

March 6

Tattooos for Christ

"From henceforth let no man trouble me: for I bear in my body the marks of the Lord Jesus."

Galatians 6:17

Prayer Requests:

Answered Prayers:

Thoughts:

March 7
He Knows Your Heart

"And they prayed, and said, Thou, Lord, which knowest the hearts of all men, ..."

Acts 1:24a

Prayer Requests:

Answered Prayers:

Thoughts:

March 8
A Walking Witness

"And all the people saw him walking and praising God:"

Acts 3:9

Prayer Requests:

Answered Prayers:

Thoughts:

March 9
Clean and Pure

"Let us draw near with a true heart in full assurance of faith, having our hearts sprinkled from an evil conscience, and our bodies washed with pure water."

Hebrews 10:22

Prayer Requests:

Answered Prayers:

Thoughts:

March 10
Given by God

"Behold, I have given him for a witness to the people, a leader and commander to the people."

Isaiah 55:4

Prayer Requests:

Answered Prayers:

Thoughts:

March 11
Witnessing to the People

"For thou shalt be His witness unto all men of what thou hast seen and heard."

Acts 22:15

Prayer Requests:

Answered Prayers:

Thoughts:

March 12

The Devil Loses by a Knockout

"And the multitudes that went before, and that followed, cried, saying, Hosanna to the son of David: Blessed is he that cometh in the name of the Lord; Hosanna in the highest."

Matthew 21:9

Prayer Requests:

Answered Prayers:

Thoughts:

March 13
No Fear

"Thou drewest near in the day that I called upon Thee: Thou saidst, Fear not."

Lamentations 3:57

Prayer Requests:

Answered Prayers:

Thoughts:

March 14
There's a Payday Someday

"Who will render to every man according to his deeds:"

Romans 2:6

Prayer Requests:

Answered Prayers:

Thoughts:

March 15
The Work of the King's Children Is Never Done

"Awake to righteousness, and sin not; for some have not the knowledge of God: I speak this to your shame."

I Corinthians 15:34

Prayer Requests:

Answered Prayers:

Thoughts:

March 16
Amazing Grace

"If so be ye have tasted that the Lord is gracious."

I Peter 2:3

Prayer Requests:

Answered Prayers:

Thoughts:

March 17
Praying Brings Results

"And when they had prayed, the place was shaken where they were assembled together; and they were all filled with the Holy Ghost, and they spake the word of God with boldness."

Acts 4:31

Prayer Requests:

Answered Prayers:

Thoughts:

March 18
God Is the Supreme Authority

"Then Peter and the other apostles answered and said, We ought to obey God rather than men."

Acts 5:29

Prayer Requests:

Answered Prayers:

Thoughts:

March 19

The Power of Christ

"But the men marvelled, saying, What manner of man is this, that even the winds and the sea obey Him!"

Matthew 8:27

Prayer Requests:

Answered Prayers:

Thoughts:

March 20
Help Is on the Way

"In the day of my trouble I will call upon Thee: for Thou wilt answer me."

Psalm 86:7

Prayer Requests:

Answered Prayers:

Thoughts:

March 21
Forever Loved

"The Lord hath appeared of old unto me, saying, Yea, I have loved thee with an everlasting love: therefore with lovingkindness have I drawn thee."

Jeremiah 31:3

Prayer Requests:

Answered Prayers:

Thoughts:

March 22

No Strings Attached

"The Lord hath appeared of old unto me, saying, Yea, I have loved thee with an everlasting love: therefore with lovingkindness have I drawn thee."

Jeremiah 31:3

Prayer Requests:

Answered Prayers:

Thoughts:

March 23
Under His Wings

"Keep me as the apple of the eye, hide me under the shadow of Thy wings,"

Psalm 17:8

Prayer Requests:

Answered Prayers:

Thoughts:

March 24
Oh, My Stars and Mars

"When I consider Thy heavens, the work of Thy fingers, the moon and the stars, which Thou hast ordained; What is man, that Thou art mindful of him? and the son of man, that Thou visitest him?"

Psalm 8:3-4

Prayer Requests:

Answered Prayers:

Thoughts:

March 25
Laughter: The Best Medicine

"A merry heart doeth good like a medicine: but a broken spirit drieth the bones. "

Proverbs 17:22

Prayer Requests:

Answered Prayers:

Thoughts:

March 26
Hold On: Help Is on the Way

"Say to them that are of a fearful heart, Be strong, fear not: behold, your God will come with vengeance, even God with a recompense; He will come and save you."

Isaiah 35:4

Prayer Requests:

Answered Prayers:

Thoughts:

March 27
Shielded by God

"Every word of God is pure: He is a shield unto them that put their trust in Him."

Proverbs 30:5

Prayer Requests:

Answered Prayers:

Thoughts:

March 28
No Greater Love

"And Jonathan said to the young man that bare his armour, Come, and let us go over unto the garrison of these uncircumcised: it may be that the Lord will work for us: for there is no restraint to the Lord to save by many or by few. And his armourbearer said unto him, Do all that is in thine heart: turn thee; behold, I am with thee according to thy heart."

I Samuel 14:6-7 (also please read I Samuel 14:8-10)

Prayer Requests:

Answered Prayers:

Thoughts:

March 29
Following His Example

"For this is thankworthy, if a man for conscience toward God endure grief, suffering wrongfully. For what glory is it, if, when ye be buffeted for your faults, ye shall take it patiently? but if, when ye do well, and suffer for it, ye take it patiently, this is acceptable with God. For even hereunto were ye called: because Christ also suffered for us, leaving us an example, that ye should follow His steps:"

I Peter 2:19-21

Prayer Requests:

Answered Prayers:

Thoughts:

March 30
Through Eyes of Faith

"Thine eyes shall see the king in His beauty: they shall behold the land that is very far off."

Isaiah 33:17

Prayer Requests:

Answered Prayers:

Thoughts:

March 31
Showers of Blessings

"And I will make them and the places round about my hill a blessing; and I will cause the shower to come down in his season; there shall be showers of blessing."

Ezekiel 34:26

Prayer Requests:

Answered Prayers:

Thoughts:

April 1
Believing Is Seeing

"Thy word is true from the beginning: and every one of Thy righteous judgments endureth for ever."

Psalm 119:160

Prayer Requests:

Answered Prayers:

Thoughts:

April 2
Never Alone

"Have not I commanded thee? Be strong and of a good courage; be not afraid, neither be thou dismayed: for the Lord thy God is with thee withersoever thou goest."

Joshua 1:9

Prayer Requests:

Answered Prayers:

Thoughts:

April 3
Why?

"And He said unto them, Why are ye troubled? and why do thoughts arise in your hearts?"

Luke 24:38

Prayer Requests:

Answered Prayers:

Thoughts:

April 4
I Heard it Through the Grapevine

"Hearing of thy love and faith, which thou hast toward the Lord Jesus and toward all saints;"

Philemon 1:5

Prayer Requests:

Answered Prayers:

Thoughts:

April 5
Faith Through the Fire

"That the trial of your faith, being much more precious than of gold that perisheth, though it be tried with fire, might be found unto praise and honour and glory at the appearing of Jesus Christ:"

I Peter 1:7

Prayer Requests:

Answered Prayers:

Thoughts:

April 6
The Alpha and Omega

"Ye are my witnesses, saith the Lord, and my servant whom I have chosen: that ye may know and believe Me, and understand that I am He: before Me there was no God formed, neither shall there be after me."

Isaiah 43:10

Prayer Requests:

Answered Prayers:

Thoughts:

April 7
He Knows All

"He revealeth the deep and secret things: He knoweth what is in the darkness, and the light dwelleth with Him."

Daniel 2:22

Prayer Requests:

Answered Prayers:

Thoughts:

April 8

It's Not What You See

"But He said unto them, I have meat to eat that ye know not of."

John 4:32

Prayer Requests:

Answered Prayers:

Thoughts:

April 9
Knowing it is True

"That thou mightest know the certainty of those things, wherein thou hast been instructed."

Luke 1:4

Prayer Requests:

Answered Prayers:

Thoughts:

April 10
Wind Beneath my Wings

"I will extol Thee, O Lord; for thou hast lifted me up, and hast not made my foes to rejoice over me."

Psalm 30:1

Prayer Requests:

Answered Prayers:

Thoughts:

April 11
Lighter than Air

"Yet I will rejoice in the Lord, I will joy in the God of my salvation. The Lord God is my strength, and He will make my feet like hinds' feet, and He will make me to walk upon mine high pl☐ ☐

Habakkuk 3:18-19

Prayer Requests:

Answered Prayers:

Thoughts:

April 12
Praying with Confidence

"Seeing then that we have a great high priest, that is passed into the heaven, Jesus the Son of God, let us hold fast our profession. For we have not an high priest which cannot be touched with the feeling of our infirmities; but was in all points tempted like as we are, yet without sin, Let us therefore come boldly unto the throne of grace, that we may obtain mercy, and find grace to help in time of need."

Hebrews 4:14-16

Prayer Requests:

Answered Prayers:

Thoughts:

April 13
Nothing Gets Past God

"For God is not unrighteous to forget your work and labour of love, which ye have shewed toward His name, in that ye have ministered to the saints, and do minister."

Hebrews 6:10

Prayer Requests:

Answered Prayers:

Thoughts:

April 14

Living with Grace

"But He giveth more grace. Wherefore He saith, God resisteth the proud, but giveth grace unto the humble."

James 4:6

Prayer Requests:

Answered Prayers:

Thoughts:

April 15
Just Do Good

"For so is the will of God, that with well doing ye may put to silence the ignorance of foolish men:"

I Peter 2:15

Prayer Requests:

Answered Prayers:

Thoughts:

April 16
"Bulldozing" for Jesus

"And Jesus said unto them, Because of your unbelief: for verily I say unto you, If ye have faith as a grain of mustard seed, ye shall say unto this mountain, Remove hence to yonder place; and it shall remove; and nothing shall be impossible unto you."

Matthew 17:20

Prayer Requests:

Answered Prayers:

Thoughts:

April 17
Only Believe

"As soon as Jesus heard the word that was spoken, He saith unto the ruler of the synagogue, Be not afraid, only believe."

Mark 5:36

Prayer Requests:

Answered Prayers:

Thoughts:

April 18
Believing unto Power

"But as many as received Him, to them gave He power to become the sons of God, even to them that believe on His name."

John 1:12

Prayer Requests:

Answered Prayers:

Thoughts:

April 19
Believe and Receive

"Therefore I say unto you, What things soever ye desire, when ye pray, believe that ye receive them, and ye shall have them."

Mark 11:24

Prayer Requests:

Answered Prayers:

Thoughts:

April 20
Belief Through Works

"If I do not the works of my Father, believe Me not. But if I do, though ye believe not Me, believe the works: that ye may know, and believe, that the Father is in Me, and I in Him."

John 10:37-38

Prayer Requests:

Answered Prayers:

Thoughts:

April 21
Precious Moments

"Unto you therefore which believe He is precious:"

I Peter 2:7(a)

Prayer Requests:

Answered Prayers:

Thoughts:

April 22
Seeing is Believing

"How then shall they call on Him in whom they have not believed? and how shall they believe in Him of whom they have not heard? and how shall they hear without a preacher?"

Romans 10:14

Prayer Requests:

Answered Prayers:

Thoughts:

April 23
He is Available

"Behold, the Lord's hand is not shortened, that it cannot save;
neither his ear heavy, that it cannot hear:"

Isaiah 59:1

Prayer Requests:

Answered Prayers:

Thoughts:

April 24

Family Resemblance

"The Spirit itself beareth witness with our spirit, that we are the children of God:"

Romans 8:16

Prayer Requests:

Answered Prayers:

Thoughts:

April 25
Speaking With Boldness

"And for me, that utterance may be given unto me, that I may open my mouth boldly, to make known the mystery of the gospel."

Ephesians 6:19

Prayer Requests:

Answered Prayers:

Thoughts:

April 26
Roaring Boldly

"The wicked flee when no man pursueth: but the righteous are bold as a lion."

Proverbs 28:1

Prayer Requests:

Answered Prayers:

Thoughts:

April 27
Opportunity is Knocking

"As we have therefore opportunity, let us do good unto all men, especially unto them who are of the household of faith."

Galatians 6:10

Prayer Requests:

Answered Prayers:

Thoughts:

April 28
No Stress

"Let not your heart be troubled: ye believe in God, believe also in Me."

John 14:1

Prayer Requests:

Answered Prayers:

Thoughts:

April 29
Called and Chosen

"Moreover whom He did predestinate, them He also called: and whom He called, them He also justified: and whom He justified, them He also glorified. What shall we then say to these things? If God be for us, who can be against us?"

Romans 8:30-31

Prayer Requests:

Answered Prayers:

Thoughts:

April 30
Full of Joy

"And these things write we unto you, that your joy may be full."

I John 1:4

Prayer Requests:

Answered Prayers:

Thoughts:

May 1
No Fear; He Is Near

"That they should seek the Lord, if haply they might feel after
Him, and find Him, though He be not far from everyone of us:"

Acts 17:27

Prayer Requests:

Answered Prayers:

Thoughts:

May 2
Going on a Treasure Hunt

"In whom are hid all the treasures of wisdom and knowledge."

Colossians 2:3

Prayer Requests:

Answered Prayers:

Thoughts:

May 3
Perfect in Him

"I in them, and Thou in Me, that they may be made perfect in one; and that the world may know that Thou has sent Me, and hast loved them, as Thou hast loved Me."

John 17:23

Prayer Requests:

Answered Prayers:

Thoughts:

May 4
Spiritual Labor

"This is a faithful saying, and these things I will that thou affirm constantly, that they which have believed in God might be careful to maintain good works. These things are good and profitable unto men."

Titus 3:8

Prayer Requests:

Answered Prayers:

Thoughts:

May 5
Godly Perfection

"That the man of God may be perfect, thoroughly furnished unto all good works."

II Timothy 3:17

Prayer Requests:

Answered Prayers:

Thoughts:

May 6
Time for Understanding

"Consider what I say; and the Lord give thee understanding in all things."

II Timothy 2:7

Prayer Requests:

Answered Prayers:

Thoughts:

May 7
You Are Glorious in Him

"And the glory which Thou gavest Me I have given them; that they may be one, even as We are one:"

John 17:22

Prayer Requests:

Answered Prayers:

Thoughts:

May 8
Everyone Is Important to God

"When they were filled, He said unto His disciples, Gather up the fragments that remain, that nothing be lost."

John 6:12

Prayer Requests:

Answered Prayers:

Thoughts:

May 9
He Keeps His Promises

"And blessed is she that believed: for there shall be a performance of those things which were told her from the Lord."

Luke 1:45

Prayer Requests:

Answered Prayers:

Thoughts:

May 10
God's Ambassador

"Then the Lord put forth His hand, and touched my mouth. And the Lord said unto me, Behold, I have put my words in thy mouth

Jeremiah 1:9

Prayer Requests:

Answered Prayers:

Thoughts:

May 11
Eternal Love

"Behold, what manner of love the Father hath bestowed upon us, that we should be called the sons of God: therefore the world knoweth us not, because it knew Him not."

I John 3:1

Prayer Requests:

Answered Prayers:

Thoughts:

May 12
He's Watching and Listening to You

"For the eyes of the Lord are over the righteous, and His ears are open unto their prayers: but the face of the Lord is against them that do evil."

I Peter 3:12

Prayer Requests:

Answered Prayers:

Thoughts:

May 13
You Are a Winner

"But thanks be to God, which giveth us the victory through our Lord Jesus Christ."

I Corinthians 15:57

Prayer Requests:

Answered Prayers:

Thoughts:

May 14
Hypocrites: Beware

"And said, If thou wilt diligently hearken to the voice of the Lord thy God, and wilt do that which is right in His sight, and wilt give ear to His commandments, and keep all His statutes, I will put none of these diseases upon thee, which I have brought upon the Egyptians: for I am the Lord that healeth thee."

Exodus 15:26

Prayer Requests:

Answered Prayers:

Thoughts:

May 15
Blessings for Obedience

"And all these blessings shall come on thee, and overtake thee, if thou shalt hearken unto the voice of the Lord thy God."

Deuteronomy 28:2

Prayer Requests:

Answered Prayers:

Thoughts:

May 16
Self-Inspection

"Now therefore thus saith the Lord of hosts; Consider your ways."

Haggai 1:5

Prayer Requests:

Answered Prayers:

Thoughts:

May 17
Serving the Master

"And the King shall answer and say unto them, Verily I say unto you, Inasmuch as ye have done it unto one of the least of these my brethern, ye have done it unto Me."

Matthew 25:40

Prayer Requests:

Answered Prayers:

Thoughts:

May 18
He's Leading the Way

"Thus saith the Lord, thy Redeemer, the Holy One of Israel; I am the Lord thy God which teacheth thee to profit, which leadeth thee by the way that thou shouldest go."

Isaiah 48:17

Prayer Requests:

Answered Prayers:

Thoughts:

May 19
Believing Unto Joy

"Whom having not seen, ye love; in whom, though now ye see Him not, yet believing, ye rejoice with joy unspeakable and full of glory:"

I Peter 1:8

Prayer Requests:

Answered Prayers:

Thoughts:

May 20
The Cost of Service

"Remember the word that I said unto you, The servant is not greater than his lord. If they have persecuted Me, they will also persecute you; if they have kept My saying, they will keep yours also."

John 15:20

Prayer Requests:

Answered Prayers:

Thoughts:

May 21
Chatting for Results

"If ye shall ask any thing in my name, I will do it."

John 14:14

Prayer Requests:

Answered Prayers:

Thoughts:

May 22
You are Free

"If the Son therefore shall make you free, ye shall be free indeed."

John 8:36

Prayer Requests:

Answered Prayers:

Thoughts:

May 23
Faithless and Fearful

"And He said unto them, Why are ye so fearful? how is it that ye have no faith? And they feared exceedingly, and said one to another, What manner of man is this, that even the wind and the sea obey Him?"

Mark 4:40-41

Prayer Requests:

Answered Prayers:

Thoughts:

May 24
He Is Great!

"For Thou art great, and doest wondrous things: Thou art God alone."

Psalm 86:10

Prayer Requests:

Answered Prayers:

Thoughts:

May 25
Take Cover

"He shall cover Thee with His feathers, and under His wings shalt thou trust: His truth shall be thy shield and buckler."

Psalm 91:4

Prayer Requests:

Answered Prayers:

Thoughts:

May 26
Glorifying through Praise

"By Him therefore let us offer the sacrifice of praise to God continually, that is, the fruit of our lips giving thanks to His name."

Hebrews 13:15

Prayer Requests:

Answered Prayers:

Thoughts:

May 27
Strangers Are Friends You Haven't Met

"Be not forgetful to entertain strangers: for thereby some have entertained angels unawares."

Hebrews 13:2

Prayer Requests:

Answered Prayers:

Thoughts:

May 28
Benefits, Benefits, Benefits

"Bless the Lord, O my soul, and forget not all His benefits:"

Psalm 103:2

Prayer Requests:

Answered Prayers:

Thoughts:

May 29
Jesus Prays for You

"Neither pray I for these alone, but for them also which shall believe on me through their word;'

John 17:20

Prayer Requests:

Answered Prayers:

Thoughts:

May 30
Power in Living

"Through God we shall do valiantly: for He it is that shall tread down our enemies."

Psalm 108:13

Prayer Requests:

Answered Prayers:

Thoughts:

May 31
Loving the Son

"Kiss the Son, lest He be angry, and ye perish from the way,
when His wrath is kindled but a little. Blessed are all they that
put their trust in Him."

Psalm 2: 12

Prayer Requests:

Answered Prayers:

Thoughts:

June 1
Walking in His Steps

"The steps of a good man are ordered by the Lord: and He delighteth in His way. Though He fall, He shall not be utterly cast down: for the Lord upholdeth Him with His hand."

Psalm 37:23-24

Prayer Requests:

Answered Prayers:

Thoughts:

June 2

A Heavenly Inheritance

"The Lord knoweth the days of the upright: and their inheritance shall be for ever."

Psalm 37:18

Prayer Requests:

Answered Prayers:

Thoughts:

June 3
An Open Door

"For a great door and effectual is opened unto me, and there are many adversaries." "Now thanks be unto God, which always causeth us to triumph in Christ, and maketh manifest the savour of His knowledge by us in every place."

I Corinthians 16:9 & II Corinthians 2:14

Prayer Requests:

Answered Prayers:

Thoughts:

June 4
Recipe for Success

"And beside this, giving all diligence, add to your faith virtue; and to virtue knowledge;"

II Peter 1:5

Prayer Requests:

Answered Prayers:

Thoughts:

June 5
Following the Master

"As ye have therefore received Christ Jesus the Lord, so walk ye in Him: Rooted and built up in Him, and stablished in the faith, as ye have been taught, abounding therein with thanksgiving."

Colossians 2:6-7

Prayer Requests:

Answered Prayers:

Thoughts:

June 6
Talk on the Basis of Your Walk

"And whatsoever we ask, we receive of Him, because we keep His commandments, and do those things that are pleasing in His sight."

I John 3:22

Prayer Requests:

Answered Prayers:

Thoughts:

June 7

We Are Victorious

*"For whatsoever is born of God overcometh the world: and this
is the victory that overcometh the world, even our faith."*

I John 5:4

Prayer Requests:

Answered Prayers:

Thoughts:

June 8
Rewards for Your Labor

"Give her of the fruit of her hands; and let her own works praise her in the gates."

Proverbs 31:31

Prayer Requests:

Answered Prayers:

Thoughts:

June 9
Not Quite Perfect...Yet!

"For there is not a just man upon earth, that doeth good, and sinneth not."

Ecclesiastes 7:20

Prayer Requests:

Answered Prayers:

Thoughts:

June 10
Staying on the Straight and Narrow

"This I say then, Walk in the Spirit, and ye shall not fulfil the lust of the flesh."

Galatians 5:16

Prayer Requests:

Answered Prayers:

Thoughts:

June 11
Held Together by God

"And Mizpah; for he said, the Lord watch between me and thee, when we are absent one from another."

Genesis 31:49

Prayer Requests:

Answered Prayers:

Thoughts:

June 12
I Am Weak, But He Is Strong

"And He said unto me, My grace is sufficient for thee: for My strength is made perfect in weakness. Most gladly therefore will I rather glory in my infirmities, that the power of Christ may rest upon me."

II Corinthians 12:9

Prayer Requests:

Answered Prayers:

Thoughts:

June 13
Perfect Love

"No man hath seen God at any time. If we love one another, God dwelleth in us, and His love is perfected in us."

I John 4:12

Prayer Requests:

Answered Prayers:

Thoughts:

June 14
Incredible Power

"The Lord on high is mightier than the noise of many waters, yea, than the mighty waves of the sea."

Psalm 93:4

Prayer Requests:

Answered Prayers:

Thoughts:

June 15
He Calls Me by Name

"Listen, O isles, unto me; and hearken, ye people, from far; The Lord hath called me from the womb; from the bowels of my mother hath He made mention of my name. And said unto me, Thou art my servant, O Israel, in whom I will be glorified."

Isaiah 49:1,3

Prayer Requests:

Answered Prayers:

Thoughts:

June 16
Let It Shine

"And God made two great lights; the greater light to rule the day, and the lesser light to rule the night: He made the stars also. He telleth the number of the stars; He calleth them all by their names."

Genesis 1:16 and Psalm 147:4

Prayer Requests:

Answered Prayers:

Thoughts:

June 17
Apart from the World

"Love not the world, neither the things that are in the world. If any man love the world, the love of the Father is not in him."

I John 2:15

Prayer Requests:

Answered Prayers:

Thoughts:

June 18
You Have a Story to Tell

"Howbeit Jesus suffered him not, but saith unto him, Go home to thy friends, and tell them how great things the Lord hath done for thee, and hath had compassion on thee."

Mark 5:19

Prayer Requests:

Answered Prayers:

Thoughts:

June 19
Working for Him

"For Thou, Lord, hast made me glad through Thy work: I will triumph in the works of Thy hands."

Psalm 92:4

Prayer Requests:

Answered Prayers:

Thoughts:

June 20
His Hand to Your Mouth

"Then the Lord put forth His hand, and touched my mouth. And the Lord said unto me, Behold, I have put my words in thy mouth."

Jeremiah 1:9

Prayer Requests:

Answered Prayers:

Thoughts:

June 21
Following Christ

"A new commandment I give unto you, That ye love one another; as I have loved you, that ye also love one another."

John 13:34

Prayer Requests:

Answered Prayers:

Thoughts:

June 22
Living Is Giving

"And it shall be in that day, that living waters shall go out from Jerusalem; half of them toward the former sea, and half of them toward the hinder sea: in summer and in winter shall it be." "But I will remove far off from you the northern army, and will drive him into a land barren and desolate, with his face toward the east sea, and his hinder part toward the utmost sea," "Go thou to the sea, and cast an hook, and take up the fish that first cometh up"

Zechariah 14:8, Joel 2:20a and Matthew 17:27b

Prayer Requests:

Answered Prayers:

Thoughts:

June 23

A Faith That Works Wonders

"And Stephen, full of faith and power, did great wonders and miracles among the people."

Acts 6:8

Prayer Requests:

Answered Prayers:

Thoughts:

June 24

You are the Light Bulb

"Ye are the light of the world."

Matthew 5:14a

Prayer Requests:

Answered Prayers:

Thoughts:

June 25
Victorious

"Nay, in all these things we are more than conquerors through Him that loved us."

Romans 8:37

Prayer Requests:

Answered Prayers:

Thoughts:

June 26
Rejoicing in Hope

"Rejoicing in hope; patient in tribulation; continuing instant in prayer;"

Romans 12:12

Prayer Requests:

Answered Prayers:

Thoughts:

June 27
It's Shouting Time

"And thou shalt rejoice in every good thing which the Lord thy God hath given unto thee,"

Deuteronomy 26:11a

Prayer Requests:

Answered Prayers:

Thoughts:

June 28
Going Fishing

"Launch out into the deep, and let down your nets for a draught."

Luke 5:4b

Prayer Requests:

Answered Prayers:

Thoughts:

.

June 29
No Matter What, God is Always There

"Nevertheless God, that comforteth those that are cast down, comforted us by the coming of Titus;"

II Corinthians 7:6

Prayer Requests:

Answered Prayers:

Thoughts:

June 30
Godly Eyes

"While we look not at the things which are seen, but at the things which are not seen: for the things which are seen are temporal; but the things which are not seen are eternal."

II Corinthians 4:18

Prayer Requests:

Answered Prayers:

Thoughts:

July 1
Moving Out of Your Comfort Zone

"And said unto him, Get thee out of thy country, and from thy kindred, and come into the land which I shall shew thee."

Acts 7:3

Prayer Requests:

Answered Prayers:

Thoughts:

July 2
God Is Everywhere You Are

"Howbeit the most High dwelleth not in temples made with hands;"

Acts 7:48a

Prayer Requests:

Answered Prayers:

Thoughts:

July 3
The Wonder of it All

"Hath not my hand made all these things?"

Acts 7:50

Prayer Requests:

Answered Prayers:

Thoughts:

July 4
Let Freedom Ring

"Let not sin therefore reign in your mortal body, that ye should obey it in the lusts thereof. Neither yield ye your members as instruments of unrighteousness unto sin: but yield yourselves unto God, as those that are alive from the dead, and your members as instruments of righteousness unto God. For sin shall not have dominion over you: for ye are not under the law, but under grace."

Romans 6:12-14

Prayer Requests:

Answered Prayers:

Thoughts:

July 5
Fruits for My Labor

"I have manifested Thy name unto the men which Thou gavest me out of the world: Thine they were, and Thou gavest them me; and they have kept thy word."

John 17:6

Prayer Requests:

Answered Prayers:

Thoughts:

July 6
Help is Near

"Thou art near, O Lord; and all thy commandments are truth."

Psalm 119:151

Prayer Requests:

Answered Prayers:

Thoughts:

July 7
Peace is Yours

"For God hath not given us the spirit of fear; but of power, and of love, and of a sound mind."

II Timothy 1:7

Prayer Requests:

Answered Prayers:

Thoughts:

July 8
He Fights Your Battles and Wins

"With him is an arm of flesh; but with us is the Lord our God to help us, and to fight our battles."

II Chronicles 32:8 (a)

Prayer Requests:

Answered Prayers:

Thoughts:

July 9
Safe and Secure

"And thou shalt be secure, because there is hope; yea thou shalt dig about thee, and thou shalt take thy rest in safety."

Job 11:18

Prayer Requests:

Answered Prayers:

Thoughts:

July 10
Meeting Your Needs

"Be not therefore like unto them: for your Father knoweth what things ye have need of, before ye ask Him."

Matthew 6:8

Prayer Requests:

Answered Prayers:

Thoughts:

July 11
In the Midst

"The just Lord is in the midst thereof; He will not do iniquity: every morning doth He bring His judgement to light, He faileth not; but the unjust knoweth no shame."

Zephaniah 3:5

Prayer Requests:

Answered Prayers:

Thoughts:

July 12
Let's Just Praise the Lord

"Praise ye the Lord: for it is good to sing praises unto our God;
for it is pleasant; and praise is comely. "

Psalm 147:1

Prayer Requests:

Answered Prayers:

Thoughts:

July 13
Walking in His Spirit

"The Spirit of the Lord is upon me, because He hath anointed me to preach the gospel to the poor; He hath sent me to heal the brokenhearted, to preach deliverance to the captives, and recovering of sight to the blind, to set at liberty them that are bruised,"

Luke 4:18

Prayer Requests:

Answered Prayers:

Thoughts:

July 14
He Lives in You

"God that made the world and all things therein, seeing that He is Lord of heaven and earth, dwelleth not in temples made with hands;"

Acts 17:24

Prayer Requests:

Answered Prayers:

Thoughts:

July 15
I Am What I Am

"But by the grace of God I am what I am: and His grace which was bestowed upon me was not in vain; but I laboured more abundantly than they all: yet not I, but the grace of God which was with me."

I Corinthians 15:10

Prayer Requests:

Answered Prayers:

Thoughts:

July 16
Borrowed Tools

"For the gifts and calling of God are without repentance."

Romans 11:29

Prayer Requests:

Answered Prayers:

Thoughts:

July 17
Serving by Example

"Let no man despise thy youth; but be thou an example of the believers, in word, in conversation, in charity, in spirit, in faith, in purity."

I Timothy 4:12

Prayer Requests:

Answered Prayers:

Thoughts:

July 18
Resting in Him

"Come unto Me, all ye that labour and are heavy laden, and I will give you rest."

Matthew 11:28

Prayer Requests:

Answered Prayers:

Thoughts:

July 19
More than Marvelous

"Praise ye the LORD. Blessed is the man that feareth the LORD, that delighteth greatly in his commandments."

Psalm 112:1

Prayer Requests:

Answered Prayers:

Thoughts:

July 20
Jesus, My Friend

"Ye are My friends, if ye do whatsoever I command you."

John 15:14

Prayer Requests:

Answered Prayers:

Thoughts:

July 21
A News Headliner

"The eyes of the Lord are upon the righteous, and His ears are open unto their cry."

Psalm 34:15

Prayer Requests:

Answered Prayers:

Thoughts:

July 22
The Master Says, "Come"

"And sent His servant at supper time to say to them that were bidden, Come; for all things are now ready."

Luke 14:17

Prayer Requests:

Answered Prayers:

Thoughts:

July 23
The Present

"This is the day which the Lord hath made; we will rejoice and be glad in it."

Psalm 118:24

Prayer Requests:

Answered Prayers:

Thoughts:

July 24
So Blessed

"Blessed are they that keep His testimonies, and that seek Him with the whole heart."

Psalm 119:2

Prayer Requests:

Answered Prayers:

Thoughts:

July 25
Trial by Fire

"That the trial of your faith, being much more precious than of gold that perisheth, though it be tried with fire, might be found unto praise and honour and glory at the appearing of Jesus Christ:"

I Peter 1:7

Prayer Requests:

Answered Prayers:

Thoughts:

July 26
Hand in Hand With God

"Draw nigh to God, and He will draw nigh to you. Cleanse your hands, ye sinners; and purify your hearts, ye double minded."

James 4:8

Prayer Requests:

Answered Prayers:

Thoughts:

July 27
Study to Remember

"But the Comforter, which is the Holy Ghost, whom the Father will send in My name, He shall teach you all things, and bring all things to your remembrance, whatsoever I have said unto you."

John 14:26

Prayer Requests:

Answered Prayers:

Thoughts:

July 28
No Worries

"Cast thy burden upon the Lord, and He shall sustain thee: He shall never suffer the righteous to be moved."

Psalm 55:22

Prayer Requests:

Answered Prayers:

Thoughts:

July 29
All Star Team

"We then, as workers together with Him, beseech you also that ye receive not the grace of God in vain."

II Corinthians 6:1

Prayer Requests:

Answered Prayers:

Thoughts:

July 30
You Have Hope

"But I will hope continually, and will yet praise Thee more and more."

Psalm 71:14

Prayer Requests:

Answered Prayers:

Thoughts:

July 31
Ready to Praise

"My lips shall greatly rejoice when I sing unto Thee; and my soul, which Thou hast redeemed."

Psalm 71:23

Prayer Requests:

Answered Prayers:

Thoughts:

August 1
A Child of the King

"But Jesus said, Suffer little children, and forbid them not, to come unto Me: for of such is the kingdom of heaven."

Matthew 19:14

Prayer Requests:

Answered Prayers:

Thoughts:

August 2
Confident, but not Cocky

"For the Lord shall be thy confidence, and shall keep thy foot from being taken."

Proverbs 3:26

Prayer Requests:

Answered Prayers:

Thoughts:

August 3
Revealing His Wonders

"Because that which may be known of God is manifest in them; for God hath shewed it unto them."

Romans 1:19

Prayer Requests:

Answered Prayers:

Thoughts:

August 4
Ordered Steps

"The steps of a good man are ordered by the Lord: and he delighteth in his way."

Psalm 37:23

Prayer Requests:

Answered Prayers:

Thoughts:

August 5
Walking With the Saviour

"The Lord is nigh unto all them that call upon Him, to all that call upon Him in truth."

Psalm 145:18

Prayer Requests:

Answered Prayers:

Thoughts:

August 6
The Invitation

"To him that overcometh will I grant to sit with Me in my throne, even as I also overcame, and am set down with my Father in His throne."

Revelation 3:21

Prayer Requests:

Answered Prayers:

Thoughts:

August 7

He Hears Your Cry and Grants the Desires of Your Heart

"I waited patiently for the Lord; and He inclined unto me, and heard my cry. He brought me up also out of an horrible pit, out of the miry clay, and set my feet upon a rock, and established my goings." "Delight thyself also in the Lord; and He shall give thee the desires of thine heart. Commit thy way unto the Lord; trust also in Him; and He shall bring it to pass."

Psalm 40:1, 2; Psalm 37:4, 5

Prayer Requests:

Answered Prayers:

Thoughts:

August 8
Keep the Faith

"And Jesus answering saith unto them, Have faith in God."

Mark 11:22

Prayer Requests:

Answered Prayers:

Thoughts:

August 9
You Are an "Overcomer"

"I can do all things through Christ which strengtheneth me."

Philippians 4:23

Prayer Requests:

Answered Prayers:

Thoughts:

August 10
Grace Under Fire

"But sanctify the Lord God in your hearts: and be ready always to give an answer to every man that asketh you a reason of the hope that is in you with meekness and fear:"

I Peter 3:15

Prayer Requests:

Answered Prayers:

Thoughts:

August 11
Will They Find You Praying?

"Then these men assembled, and found Daniel praying and making supplication before his God."

Daniel 6:11

Prayer Requests:

Answered Prayers:

Thoughts:

August 12
Worshipping in Prayer

"After this manner therefore pray ye: Our Father which art in heaven, Hallowed be Thy name."

Matthew 6:9

Prayer Requests:

Answered Prayers:

Thoughts:

August 13
Surrendering in Prayer

"Thy kingdom come. Thy will be done in earth, as it is in heaven."

Matthew 6:10

Prayer Requests:

Answered Prayers:

Thoughts:

August 14
Petitioning in Prayer

"Give us this day our daily bread. And forgive us our debts, as we forgive our debtors. And lead us not into temptation, but deliver us from evil: For Thine is the kingdom, and the power, and the glory, for ever. Amen."

Matthew 6:11-13

Prayer Requests:

Answered Prayers:

Thoughts:

August 15
Confessing and Forgiving in Prayer

"And forgive us our debts, as we forgive our debtors."

Matthew 6:12

Prayer Requests:

Answered Prayers:

Thoughts:

August 16
Thanking God in Prayer

"For Thine is the kingdom, and the power, and the glory, for ever. Amen."

Matthew 6:13b

Prayer Requests:

Answered Prayers:

Thoughts:

August 17
The Time Is Now

"Sow to yourselves in righteousness, reap in mercy; break up your fallow ground: for it is time to seek the Lord, till He come and rain righteousness upon you."

Hosea 10:12

Prayer Requests:

Answered Prayers:

Thoughts:

August 18
Tilling Ground

"Verily, verily, I say unto thee, We speak that we do know, and testify that we have seen; and ye receive not our witness."

John 3:11

Prayer Requests:

Answered Prayers:

Thoughts:

August 19
Casting Your Cares Into the Sea of Forgetfulness

"Casting all your care upon Him; for He careth for you."

I Peter 5:7

Prayer Requests:

Answered Prayers:

Thoughts:

August 20
Maintaining Good Works

"This is a faithful saying, and these things I will that thou affirm constantly, that they which have believed in God might be careful to maintain good works. These things are good and profitable unto men."

Titus 3:8

Prayer Requests:

Answered Prayers:

Thoughts:

August 21
Trusting His Blessings

"Blessed is the man that trusteth in the LORD, and whose hope the Lord is."

Jeremiah 17:7

Prayer Requests:

Answered Prayers:

Thoughts:

August 22
Speaking with Power

"Thy word is a lamp unto my feet, and a light unto my path."

Psalm 119:105

Prayer Requests:

Answered Prayers:

Thoughts:

August 23
A Powerful Witness

"The woman then left her waterpot, and went her way into the city, and saith to the men, Come, see a man, which told me all things that ever I did: is not this the Christ?"

John 4:28-29

Prayer Requests:

Answered Prayers:

Thoughts:

August 24
Be Forceful

"But sanctify the Lord God in your hearts: and be ready always to give an answer to every man that asketh you a reason of the hope that is in you with meekness and fear:"

I Peter 3:15

Prayer Requests:

Answered Prayers:

Thoughts:

August 25
Thanks Be to God!

"A man can receive nothing, except it be given him from heaven."

John 3:27b

Prayer Requests:

Answered Prayers:

Thoughts:

August 26
Seeing God

"Blessed are the pure in heart: for they shall see God."

Matthew 5:8

Prayer Requests:

Answered Prayers:

Thoughts:

August 27
Walking the Talk

"But as for me, I will walk in mine integrity: redeem me, and be merciful unto me. My foot standeth in an even place: in the congregations will I bless the Lord."

Psalm 26:11-12

Prayer Requests:

Answered Prayers:

Thoughts:

August 28
Pure in Him

"Beloved, now are we the sons of God, and it doth not yet appear what we shall be: but we know that, when He shall appear, we shall be like Him; for we shall see Him as He is. And every man that hath this hope in him purifieth himself, even as He is pure."

I John 3:2-3

Prayer Requests:

Answered Prayers:

Thoughts:

August 29
Oh, How He Loves You!

"Wherefore, if God so clothe the grass of the field, which to day is, and to morrow is cast into the oven, shall He not much more clothe you, O ye of little faith?"

Matthew 6:30

Prayer Requests:

Answered Prayers:

Thoughts:

August 30
His Promises are True!

"Blessed be the Lord, that hath given rest unto His people Israel, according to all that He promised: there hath not failed one word of all His good promise, which He promised by the hand of Moses His servant."

I Kings 8:56 and Malachi 3:6a

Prayer Requests:

Answered Prayers:

Thoughts:

August 31
The Power of Faith

"Wherefore I also, after I heard of your faith in the Lord Jesus, and love unto all the saints, Cease not to give thanks for you, making mention of you in my prayers;"

Ephesians 1:15-16

Prayer Requests:

Answered Prayers:

Thoughts:

September 1
Words of Life

"It is the spirit that quickeneth; the flesh profiteth nothing: the words that I speak unto you, they are spirit, and they are life."

John 6:63

Prayer Requests:

Answered Prayers:

Thoughts:

September 2
God Knows Me

"The Lord is good, a strong hold in the day of trouble; and He knoweth them that trust in Him."

Nahum 1:7

Prayer Requests:

Answered Prayers:

Thoughts:

September 3
Follow the Leader

"So the Lord alone did lead him, and there was no strange god with him."

Deuteronomy 32:12

Prayer Requests:

Answered Prayers:

Thoughts:

September 4
Blessings for the Just

"Blessings are upon the head of the just:"

Proverbs 10:6a

Prayer Requests:

Answered Prayers:

Thoughts:

September 5
I Am Not Ashamed

"O keep my soul, and deliver me: let me not be ashamed; for I put my trust in Thee."

Psalm 25:20

Prayer Requests:

Answered Prayers:

Thoughts:

September 6
Touched by an Angel

"Yea, whiles I was speaking in prayer, even the man Gabriel, whom I had seen in the vision at the beginning, being caused to fly swiftly, touched me about the time of the evening oblation."

Daniel 9:21

Prayer Requests:

Answered Prayers:

Thoughts:

September 7
The Rewards of Belief

"And blessed is she that believed: for there shall be a performance of those things which were told her from the Lord."

Luke 1:45

Prayer Requests:

Answered Prayers:

Thoughts:

September 8
No Fear; Only Believe

"As soon as Jesus heard the word that was spoken, He saith unto the ruler of the synagogue, Be not afraid, only believe."

Mark 5:36

Prayer Requests:

Answered Prayers:

Thoughts:

September 9
Timely Words

"For the Holy Ghost shall teach you in the same hour what ye ought to say."

Luke 12:12

Prayer Requests:

Answered Prayers:

Thoughts:

September 10
Fear Not

"Fear not, little flock; for it is your Father's good pleasure to give you the kingdom."

Luke 12:32

Prayer Requests:

Answered Prayers:

Thoughts:

September 11
He Is in Control

"I know that Thou canst do every thing, and that no thought can be withholden from Thee."

Job 42:2

Prayer Requests:

Answered Prayers:

Thoughts:

September 12
Where Is Your Treasure?

"For where your treasure is, there will your heart be also."

Luke 12:34

Prayer Requests:

Answered Prayers:

Thoughts:

September 13
Be Prepared

"Be ye therefore ready also: for the Son of man cometh at an hour when ye think not."

Luke 12:40

Prayer Requests:

Answered Prayers:

Thoughts:

September 14
You Are an Example

"So that ye were ensamples to all that believe"

I Thessalonians 1:7

Prayer Requests:

Answered Prayers:

Thoughts:

September 15
Witnessing Unto All the World

"Go ye therefore, and teach all nations, baptizing them in the name of the Father, and of the Son, and of the Holy Ghost: Teaching them to observe all things whatsoever I have commanded you: and, lo, I am with you alway, even unto the end of the world. Amen."

Matthew 28:19-20

Prayer Requests:

Answered Prayers:

Thoughts:

September 16
Receiving His Word

"For this cause also thank we God without ceasing, because, when ye received the word of God which ye heard of us, ye received it not as the word of men, but as it is in truth, the word of God, which effectually worketh also in you that believe."

I Thessalonians 2:13

Prayer Requests:

Answered Prayers:

Thoughts:

September 17
Lift Up Your Hands

"Lift up your hands in the sanctuary, and bless the Lord. "

Psalm 134:2

Prayer Requests:

Answered Prayers:

Thoughts:

September 18
The Power of Pure Thinking

"Finally, brethren, whatsoever things are true, whatsoever things are honest, whatsoever things are just, whatsoever things are pure, whatsoever things are lovely, whatsoever things are of good report; if there be any virtue, and if there be any praise, think on these things."

Philippians 4:8

Prayer Requests:

Answered Prayers:

Thoughts:

September 19

The Time Is Yours

"Thou art come to the kingdom for such a time as this"

Esther 4:14b

Prayer Requests:

Answered Prayers:

Thoughts:

September 20
Follow That Which Is Good

"See that none render evil for evil unto any man; but ever follow that which is good, both among yourselves, and to all men."

I Thessalonians 5:15

Prayer Requests:

Answered Prayers:

Thoughts:

September 21
Punishment Exists for Those Who Know Not God

"That they all might be damned who believed not the truth, but had pleasure in unrighteousness."

II Thessalonians 2:12

Prayer Requests:

Answered Prayers:

Thoughts:

September 22
God's Teachings Produce Results

"Teach me, and I will hold my tongue: and cause me to understand wherein I have erred."

Job 6:24

Prayer Requests:

Answered Prayers:

Thoughts:

September 23
Benefits of Instruction

"Give instruction to a wise man, and he will be yet wiser: teach a just man, and he will increase in learning."

Proverbs 9:9

Prayer Requests:

Answered Prayers:

Thoughts:

September 24
Expensive Real Estate

"For we know that if our earthly house of this tabernacle were dissolved, we have a building of God, an house not made with hands, eternal in the heavens."

II Corinthians 5:1

Prayer Requests:

Answered Prayers:

Thoughts:

September 25
You Have Boundaries

"For the love of Christ constraineth us;"

II Corinthians 5:14a

Prayer Requests:

Answered Prayers:

Thoughts:

September 26
Worship the Lord

"Let them praise the name of the Lord: for His name alone is excellent; His glory is above the earth and heaven. "

Psalm 148:13

Prayer Requests:

Answered Prayers:

Thoughts:

September 27
Commit to Him

"Commit thy way unto the Lord; trust also in Him; and He shall bring it to pass. "

Psalm 37:5

Prayer Requests:

Answered Prayers:

Thoughts:

September 28
Petition God

"If any of you lack wisdom, let him ask of God, that giveth to all men liberally, and upbraideth not; and it shall be given him. But let him ask in faith, nothing wavering. For he that wavereth is like a wave of the sea driven with the wind and tossed."

James 1:5-6

Prayer Requests:

Answered Prayers:

Thoughts:

September 29
Confess to Possess Great Power

"I acknowledged my sin unto Thee, and mine iniquity have I not hid. I said, I will confess my transgressions unto the LORD; and Thou forgavest the iniquity of my sin. Selah."

Psalm 32:5

Prayer Requests:

Answered Prayers:

Thoughts:

September 30
Thank You, Lord

"Now thanks be unto God, which always causeth us to triumph in Christ, and maketh manifest the savour of His knowledge by us in every place."

II Corinthians 2:14

Prayer Requests:

Answered Prayers:

Thoughts:

October 1
He Will Provide

"And He said unto them, When I sent you without purse, and scrip, and shoes, lacked ye any thing? And they said, Nothing."

Luke 22:35

Prayer Requests:

Answered Prayers:

Thoughts:

October 2
Peace in His Midst

"And as they thus spake, Jesus himself stood in the midst of them, and saith unto them, Peace be unto you."

Luke 24:36

Prayer Requests:

Answered Prayers:

Thoughts:

October 3
He Gives Understanding

"Then opened He their understanding, that they might understand the scriptures,"

Luke 24:45

Prayer Requests:

Answered Prayers:

Thoughts:

October 4
You Have a Job to Do

"And that repentance and remission of sins should be preached in His name among all nations, beginning at Jerusalem."

Luke 24:47

Prayer Requests:

Answered Prayers:

Thoughts:

October 5
The Way is Prepared

"As it is written in the prophets, Behold, I send my messenger before thy face, which shall prepare thy way before thee."

Mark 1:2

Prayer Requests:

Answered Prayers:

Thoughts:

October 6
Be a Good Neighbor

"Which now of these three, thinkest thou, was neighbour unto him that fell among the thieves? And He said, he that shewed mercy on him. Then said Jesus unto him, Go, and do thou likewise."

Luke 10:36-37

Prayer Requests:

Answered Prayers:

Thoughts:

October 7
Heavenly Eyes

"And He turned Him unto His disciples, and said privately,
Blessed are the eyes which see the things that ye see:"

Luke 10:23

Prayer Requests:

Answered Prayers:

Thoughts:

October 8
He Feels Your Pain

"And there came a leper to him, beseeching him, and kneeling down to him, and saying unto him, If thou wilt, thou canst make me clean. And Jesus, moved with compassion, put forth his hand, and touched him, and saith unto him, I will; be thou clean."

Mark 1:40-41

Prayer Requests:

Answered Prayers:

Thoughts:

October 9
You Are in the Family of God

"For whosoever shall do the will of God, the same is My brother, and My sister, and mother."

Mark 3:35

Prayer Requests:

Answered Prayers:

Thoughts:

October 10
He Speaks Peace to You

"And immediately He talked with them, and saith unto them, Be of good cheer: it is I; be not afraid."

Mark 6:50b

Prayer Requests:

Answered Prayers:

Thoughts:

October 11
God Specializes in the Impossible

"And Jesus looking upon them saith, With men it is impossible, but not with God: for with God all things are possible."

Mark 10:27

Prayer Requests:

Answered Prayers:

Thoughts:

October 12
Hundredfold Reward

"And Jesus answered and said, Verily I say unto you, There is no man that hath left house, or brethren, or sisters, or father, or mother, or wife, or children, or lands, for my sake, and the gospel's, But he shall receive an hundredfold now in this time, houses, and brethren, and sisters, and mothers, and children, and lands, with persecutions; and in the world to come eternal life."

Mark 10:29-30

Prayer Requests:

Answered Prayers:

Thoughts:

October 13
Some Won't Listen—Tell Them Anyway

"For the preaching of the cross is to them that perish foolishness; but unto us which are saved it is the power of God."

I Corinthians 1:18

Prayer Requests:

Answered Prayers:

Thoughts:

October 14
Faith in God

"That your faith should not stand in the wisdom of men, but in the power of God."

I Corinthians 2:5

Prayer Requests:

Answered Prayers:

Thoughts:

October 15
He Loves You

"And while they abode in Galilee, Jesus said unto them, The Son of man shall be betrayed into the hands of men:"

Matthew 17:22

Prayer Requests:

Answered Prayers:

Thoughts:

October 16
Love Your Neighbor

"Thou shalt love thy neighbour as thyself."

Matthew 19:19b

Prayer Requests:

Answered Prayers:

Thoughts:

October 17
Be Not Ashamed

"For the scripture saith, Whosoever believeth on Him shall not be ashamed."

Romans 10:11

Prayer Requests:

Answered Prayers:

Thoughts:

October 18
Tarry Until You Are Plugged into God

"And, behold, I send the promise of my Father upon you: but tarry ye in the city of Jerusalem, until ye be endued with power from on high."

Luke 24:49

Prayer Requests:

Answered Prayers:

Thoughts:

October 19
He Has Free Gifts to Give You

"Now we have received, not the spirit of the world, but the spirit which is of God; that we might know the things that are freely given to us of God."

I Corinthians 2:12

Prayer Requests:

Answered Prayers:

Thoughts:

October 20

Watch Where Your Feet Take You

"Know ye not that ye are the temple of God, and that the Spirit of God dwelleth in you?"

I Corinthians 3:16

Prayer Requests:

Answered Prayers:

Thoughts:

October 21
The Master Wants You

"The Master is come, and calleth for thee."

John 11:28b

Prayer Requests:

Answered Prayers:

Thoughts:

October 22
You Are God's Gardener

Now He that planteth and He that watereth are one: and every man shall receive his own reward according to his own labour. "

I Corinthians 3:8

Prayer Requests:

Answered Prayers:

Thoughts:

October 23
The Holy Spirit Speaks

"But when they shall lead you, and deliver you up, take no thought beforehand what ye shall speak, neither do ye premeditate: but whatsoever shall be given you in that hour, that speak ye: for it is not ye that speak, but the Holy Ghost."

Mark 13:11

Prayer Requests:

Answered Prayers:

Thoughts:

October 24
Love God

"And to love Him with all the heart, and with all the understanding, and with all the soul, and with all the strength, and to love his neighbour as himself, is more than all whole burnt offerings and sacrifices."

Mark 12:33

Prayer Requests:

Answered Prayers:

Thoughts:

October 25
Pray Away Temptation

"Watch ye and pray, lest ye enter into temptation. The spirit truly is ready, but the flesh is weak."

Mark 14:38

Prayer Requests:

Answered Prayers:

Thoughts:

Ocotober 26
He Calls You

"And they call the blind man, saying unto him, Be of good comfort, rise; He calleth thee."

Mark 10:49b

Prayer Requests:

Answered Prayers:

Thoughts:

October 27
More of Him, Less of Me

"He must increase, but I must decrease."

John 3:30

Prayer Requests:

Answered Prayers:

Thoughts:

October 28
Giving in His Name

"And whosoever shall give to drink unto one of these little ones a cup of cold water only in the name of a disciple, verily I say unto you, he shall in no wise lose his reward."

Matthew 10:42

Prayer Requests:

Answered Prayers:

Thoughts:

October 29
A Servant to All

"And whosoever of you will be the chiefest, shall be servant of all."

Mark 10:44

Prayer Requests:

Answered Prayers:

Thoughts:

October 30
Start Your Day Off Right

"And in the morning, rising up a great while before day, He went out, and departed into a solitary place, and there prayed."

Mark 1:35

Prayer Requests:

Answered Prayers:

Thoughts:

October 31
Have Faith in God

"And Jesus answering saith unto them, Have faith in God."

Mark 11:22

Prayer Requests:

Answered Prayers:

Thoughts:

November 1
Love the Lord With All Your Heart

"And thou shalt love the Lord thy God with all thy heart, and with all thy soul, and with all thy mind, and with all thy strength: this is the first commandment."

Mark 12:30

Prayer Requests:

Answered Prayers:

Thoughts:

November 2
His Words Are True

"Heaven and earth shall pass away: but My words shall not pass away."

Mark 13:31

Prayer Requests:

Answered Prayers:

Thoughts:

November 3
Our Faith Is a Gift and a Treasure

"That is, that I may be comforted together with you by the mutual faith both of you and me."

Romans 1:12

Prayer Requests:

Answered Prayers:

Thoughts:

November 4
A Strong Faith

"He staggered not at the promise of God through unbelief; but was strong in faith, giving glory to God; And being fully persuaded that, what He had promised, He was able also to perform."

Romans 4:20, 21

Prayer Requests:

Answered Prayers:

Thoughts:

November 5
He Is Life

"In Him was life; and the life was the light of men."

John 1:4

Prayer Requests:

Answered Prayers:

Thoughts:

November 6
Sin Need Not Win Again

"The next day John seeth Jesus coming unto him, and saith, Behold the Lamb of God, which taketh away the sin of the world."

John 1:29

Prayer Requests:

Answered Prayers:

Thoughts:

November 7
The Justification of Faith

"Therefore being justified by faith, we have peace with God through our Lord Jesus Christ:"

Romans 5:1

Prayer Requests:

Answered Prayers:

Thoughts:

November 8
Hope

"By whom also we have access by faith into this grace wherein we stand, and rejoice in hope of the glory of God."

Romans 5:2

Prayer Requests:

Answered Prayers:

Thoughts:

November 9
Everyone Is Precious in His Sight

"When they were filled, He said unto His disciples, Gather up the fragments that remain, that nothing be lost."

John 6:12

Prayer Requests:

Answered Prayers:

Thoughts:

November 10
We Love Him Because He Is Good to Us

"Jesus answered them and said, Verily, Verily, I say unto you,
Ye seek me, not because ye saw the miracles, but because ye did
eat of the loaves, and were filled."

John 6:26

Prayer Requests:

Answered Prayers:

Thoughts:

November 11
Witnessing Unto Belief

"And many of the Samaritans of that city believed on Him for the saying of the woman, which testified, He told me all that ever I did."

John 4:39

Prayer Requests:

Answered Prayers:

Thoughts:

November 12
You Are His Hands and Feet Extended

"And went to him, and bound up his wounds, pouring in oil and wine, and set him on his own beast, and brought him to an inn, and took care of him."

Luke 10:34

Prayer Requests:

Answered Prayers:

Thoughts:

November 13
A Heart on Fire

"And they said one to another, Did not our heart burn within us, while He talked with us by the way, and while He opened to us the scriptures?"

Luke 24:32

Prayer Requests:

Answered Prayers:

Thoughts:

November 14
Speaking His Words

"Then the Lord put forth His hand, and touched my mouth. And the Lord said unto me, Behold, I have put My words in thy mouth."

Jeremiah 1:9

Prayer Requests:

Answered Prayers:

Thoughts:

November 15
Seeking With Your Heart

"But if from thence thou shalt seek the Lord thy God, thou shalt find Him, if thou seek Him with all thy heart and with all thy soul."

Deuteronomy 4:29

Prayer Requests:

Answered Prayers:

Thoughts:

November 16
You Are Hot Stuff

"Who maketh His angels spirits; His ministers a flaming fire:"

Psalm 104:4

Prayer Requests:

Answered Prayers:

Thoughts:

November 17
Glory Awaits

"For I reckon that the sufferings of this present time are not worthy to be compared with the glory which shall be revealed in us."

Romans 8:18

Prayer Requests:

Answered Prayers:

Thoughts:

November 18

You Are on the Winning Side

"What shall we then say to these things? If God be for us, who can be against us?"

Romans 8:31

Prayer Requests:

Answered Prayers:

Thoughts:

November 19
Limitless Resources

"For of Him, and through Him, and to Him, are all things: to whom be glory for ever. Amen."

Romans 11:36

Prayer Requests:

Answered Prayers:

Thoughts:

November 20
Hope Is in Christ

"Now the God of hope fill you with all joy and peace in believing, that ye may abound in hope, through the power of the Holy Ghost."

Romans 15:13

Prayer Requests:

Answered Prayers:

Thoughts:

November 21
Battling the Devil Through the Strength of Christ

"And the God of peace shall bruise Satan under your feet shortly. The grace of our Lord Jesus Christ be with you. Amen."

Romans 16:20

Prayer Requests:

Answered Prayers:

Thoughts:

November 22
Speak Always

"Preach the word; be instant in season, out of season; reprove, rebuke, exhort with all longsuffering and doctrine."

II Timothy 4:2

Prayer Requests:

Answered Prayers:

Thoughts:

November 23
The Wisdom of Youth

"...but I thy servant fear the Lord from my youth."

I Kings 18:12b

Prayer Requests:

Answered Prayers:

Thoughts:

November 24
Loving Like Christ

"Hereby perceive we the love of God, because He laid down His life for us: and we ought to lay down our lives for the brethren."
I John 3:16

Prayer Requests:

Answered Prayers:

Thoughts:

November 25
Give it All You Got

"Not with eyeservice, as menpleasers; but as the servants of Christ, doing the will of God from the heart;"

Ephesians 6:6

Prayer Requests:

Answered Prayers:

Thoughts:

November 26
Abstain Unto Holiness

"Dearly beloved, I beseech you as strangers and pilgrims, abstain from fleshly lusts, which war against the soul;"

I Peter 2:11

Prayer Requests:

Answered Prayers:

Thoughts:

November 27
The Secret to Riches

"By humility and the fear of the Lord are riches, and honour, and life."

Proverbs 22:4

Prayer Requests:

Answered Prayers:

Thoughts:

November 28
Living By Faith

"For therein is the righteousness of God revealed from faith to faith: as it is written, The just shall live by faith."

Romans 1:17

Prayer Requests:

Answered Prayers:

Thoughts:

November 29
You Are Important to God

"So being affectionately desirous of you, we were willing to have imparted unto you, not the gospel of God only, but also our own souls, because ye were dear unto us."

I Thessalonians 2:8

Prayer Requests:

Answered Prayers:

Thoughts:

November 30
A Strong Hold

"Now unto Him that is able to keep you from falling, and to present you faultless before the presence of His glory with exceeding joy,"

Jude 24

Prayer Requests:

Answered Prayers:

Thoughts:

December 1
He Chooses You

"Thus saith the Lord, the Redeemer of Israel, and His Holy One, to Him whom man despiseth, to Him whom the nation abhorreth, to a servant of rulers, Kings shall see and arise, princes also shall worship, because of the Lord that is faithful, and the Holy One of Israel, and He shall choose thee."

Isaiah 49:7

Prayer Requests:

Answered Prayers:

Thoughts:

December 2
The Lord Will Prepare a Way

"Behold, I will send my messenger, and he shall prepare the way before me: and the Lord, whom ye seek, shall suddenly come to His temple, even the messenger of the covenant, whom ye delight in: behold, He shall come, saith the Lord of hosts."

Malachi 3:1

Prayer Requests:

Answered Prayers:

Thoughts:

December 3
Do Not Be Afraid

"Behold, God is my salvation; I will trust, and not be afraid: for the Lord Jehovah is my strength and my song; He also is become my salvation."

Isaiah 12:2

Prayer Requests:

Answered Prayers:

Thoughts:

December 4

The Secret to Blessings

"Blessed is the man whose strength is in Thee; in whose heart are the ways of them."

Psalm 84:5

Prayer Requests:

Answered Prayers:

Thoughts:

December 5
A Purpose to Strive For

"That men may know that Thou, whose name alone is Jehovah, art the Most High over all the earth."

Psalm 83:18

Prayer Requests:

Answered Prayers:

Thoughts:

December 6
Today

"To every thing there is a season, and a time to every purpose under the heaven:"

Ecclesiastes 3:1

Prayer Requests:

Answered Prayers:

Thoughts:

December 7
Studying Pays

"Study to shew thyself approved unto God, a workman that needeth not to be ashamed, rightly dividing the word of truth."

II Timothy 2:15

Prayer Requests:

Answered Prayers:

Thoughts:

December 8
Victorious in Battle

"Be sober, be vigilant; because your adversary the devil, as a roaring lion, walketh about, seeking whom he may devour:"

I Peter 5:8

Prayer Requests:

Answered Prayers:

Thoughts:

December 9
Living in Peace

"These things I have spoken unto you, that in Me ye might have peace. In the world ye shall have tribulation: but be of good cheer; I have overcome the world."

John 16:33

Prayer Requests:

Answered Prayers:

Thoughts:

December 10
Fit to Serve

*"Herein is our love made perfect, that we may have boldness in
the day of judgment: because as He is, so are we in this world."*
I John 4:17

Prayer Requests:

Answered Prayers:

Thoughts:

December 11
He Is Powerful, Wise and in Control

"He hath made the earth by his power, He hath established the world by His wisdom, and hath stretched out the heavens by His discretion."

Jeremiah 10:12

Prayer Requests:

Answered Prayers:

Thoughts:

December 12
Heavenly Strength

"I can do all things through Christ which strengtheneth me."
                                                    Philippians 4:13

Prayer Requests:

Answered Prayers:

Thoughts:

December 13
You Are Not Alone

"for He hath said, I will never leave thee, nor forsake thee."

Hebrews 13:5b

Prayer Requests:

Answered Prayers:

Thoughts:

December 14
God Is Greater

"Ye are of God, little children, and have overcome them: because greater is He that is in you, than he that is in the world."

I John 4:4

Prayer Requests:

Answered Prayers:

Thoughts:

December 15
The Great Defender

"But let all those that put their trust in Thee rejoice: let them ever shout for joy, because Thou defendest them: let them also that love Thy name be joyful in Thee."

Psalm 5:11

Prayer Requests:

Answered Prayers:

Thoughts:

December 16

He Lights My Way

"For the Lord God is a sun and shield: the Lord will give grace and glory: no good thing will He withhold from them that walk uprightly."

Psalm 84:11

Prayer Requests:

Answered Prayers:

Thoughts:

December 17
Using His Gifts

"And I was afraid, and went and hid thy talent in the earth: lo, there thou hast that is thine."

Matthew 25:25

Prayer Requests:

Answered Prayers:

Thoughts:

December 18
Two Is a Powerful Number

"For where two or three are gathered together in My name, there am I in the midst of them."

Matthew 18:20

Prayer Requests:

Answered Prayers:

Thoughts:

December 19
Speaking With the Master

"The word of the Lord came again unto me, saying,"

Ezekiel 27:1

Prayer Requests:

Answered Prayers:

Thoughts:

December 20
Faith Walkers

"For we walk by faith, not by sight:"

II Corinthians 5:7

Prayer Requests:

Answered Prayers:

Thoughts:

December 21
Benefits Beyond Belief

"But Godliness with contentment is great gain."

I Timothy 6:6

Prayer Requests:

Answered Prayers:

Thoughts:

December 22
Friendship's Gift

"One is so near to another, that no air can come between them. They are joined one to another, they stick together, that they cannot be sundered."

Job 41:16, 17

Prayer Requests:

Answered Prayers:

Thoughts:

December 23
Applying the Promises of God to Your Life

"Having therefore these promises, dearly beloved, let us cleanse ourselves from all filthiness of the flesh and spirit, perfecting holiness in the fear of God."

II Corinthians 7:1

Prayer Requests:

Answered Prayers:

Thoughts:

December 24

Somebody's Praying for You

"I thank God, whom I serve from my forefathers with pure conscience, that without ceasing I have remembrance of thee in my prayers night and day;"

II Timothy 1:3

Prayer Requests:

Answered Prayers:

Thoughts:

December 25
Glory to God in the Highest

"For unto you is born this day in the city of David a Saviour, which is Christ the Lord."

Luke 2:11

Prayer Requests:

Answered Prayers:

Thoughts:

December 26
Spiritual Exercise

"For bodily exercise profiteth little: but Godliness is profitable unto all things, having promise of the life that now is, and of that which is to come."

I Timothy 4:8

Prayer Requests:

Answered Prayers:

Thoughts:

December 27
Producing Good Works

"That ye might walk worthy of the Lord unto all pleasing, being fruitful in every good work, and increasing in the knowledge of God;"

Colossians 1:10

Prayer Requests:

Answered Prayers:

Thoughts:

December 28
The Link of Sharing

"Bear ye one another's burdens, and so fulfil the law of Christ."

Galatians 6:2

Prayer Requests:

Answered Prayers:

Thoughts:

December 29
It Is All Good

"And we know that all things work together for good to them that love God, to them who are the called according to his purpose."

Romans 8:28

Prayer Requests:

Answered Prayers:

Thoughts:

December 30
Serving with Gladness

"Serve the Lord with gladness: come before His presence with singing."

Psalm 100:2

Prayer Requests:

Answered Prayers:

Thoughts:

December 31
The Divine Appointment

"And He must needs go through Samaria."

John 4:4

Prayer Requests:

Answered Prayers:

Thoughts: